Noah Porte

The two-hundredth birthday of bishop George Berkeley

A discourse given at Yale College on the 12th of March, 1885

Noah Porter

The two-hundredth birthday of bishop George Berkeley
A discourse given at Yale College on the 12th of March, 1885

ISBN/EAN: 9783743337688

Manufactured in Europe, USA, Canada, Australia, Japa

Cover: Foto ©Thomas Meinert / pixelio.de

Manufactured and distributed by brebook publishing software (www.brebook.com)

Noah Porter

The two-hundredth birthday of bishop George Berkeley

ERRATUM.

Page 69. For "Rector Williams, etc.," read "President Clap in his history of Yale College expresses the opinion that 'this College will always retain a most grateful sense of his generosity and merits; and probably a favorable opinion of his idea of *material substance* as not consisting in an unknown and inconceivable *substratum* but in a *stated union and combination of sensible ideas* excited from without by some *intelligent* Being.'"

THE TWO-HUNDREDTH BIRTHDAY OF

BISHOP GEORGE BERKELEY

A DISCOURSE GIVEN AT YALE COLLEGE ON THE 12TH OF MARCH, 1885

BY

NOAH PORTER

NEW-YORK
CHARLES SCRIBNER'S SONS
1885

Copyright, 1885, by Charles Scribner's Sons.

THIS VOLUME IS INSCRIBED

TO

THOMAS MARCH CLARK, D. D., D. C. L.

AND

WILLIAM INGRAHAM KIP, D. D., LL. D.

CLASSMATES OF THE WRITER AT YALE,

WHO, AS BISHOPS OF
RHODE ISLAND AND CALIFORNIA,
ARE ONE WITH HIM IN HONORING
THE MEMORY OF

BERKELEY.

PREFACE.

The substance of the following discourse was given at Yale College on the 12th of March, 1885, in commemoration of the 200th birthday of the distinguished and excellent Berkeley. Most of the materials were taken from the elaborate "Life and Letters" by Professor Alexander Campbell Fraser, M. A., Oxford, 1871; and the more brief but excellent sketch by the same author in Knight's "Philosophical Classics," Edinburgh, 1881. The design of the writer was to present in a compact and somewhat popular form the most important facts in Berkeley's history, that he might do something to keep his memory fresh and fragrant in the minds of studious and thoughtful men and women of the present generation. With the same desire he gives this discourse to the public, with the added wish that what he has written may also incite some of his readers to a thorough study of Berkeley's Philosophy. No better discipline to clear and sharp thinking, and at the same time to noble aims and aspirations, can be furnished than can be gained by a study of Berkeley's life and opinions. The exhaustive biographies by Professor Fraser, already named, are all that are needed for the study of his life. The "Selections from Berkeley, with an introduction and notes for the use of Students in the Universities," Oxford, 1874, by the same writer, and the admirably annotated edition of the "Treatise concerning the Principles of Human Knowledge," by the late Professor and Vice-Provost Charles P. Krauth, D. D., Philadelphia, 1874, are all that are required for the intelligent study of Berkeley's writings.

It is always refreshing, and sometimes instructive, to turn from Kant or Hegel, and even from Lotze and Wundt, to the sharp and sparkling, if he is now and then the paradoxical and pertinacious Berkeley.

The memory of Berkeley will always be fresh

Preface. vii

and fragrant with all generous and thoughtful souls. The facts are not without interest, that Berkeley's name is connected with one of the most interesting and delightful points of land that looks out upon the stormy Atlantic towards the "still-vexed Bermoothes," where he hoped to locate his college, and has also been attached to the beautiful site of the University of California, which commands the golden gate that opens into the great Pacific.

Not only has his own prophecy been fulfilled— "Westward the course of Empire takes its way," but his name has also gone westward to hallow and inspire all those enterprises of education and religion such as he desired to initiate, which distinguish and glorify that greater kingdom of God, which sooner or later shall encircle " the round world," and bless all those who dwell therein.

Yale College, April, 1885.

GEORGE BERKELEY, dean and bishop, was born two hundred years ago this very day. His character was unique for unselfish enthusiasm in a corrupt and selfish time; his contributions to the literature and philosophy of his generation were timely and effective; his influence upon the speculation and culture of the world continues to be felt and acknowledged; his interest in Ireland and America is still remembered with grateful regard. For all these reasons his *two-hundredth birthday* deserves to be noticed with a grateful benediction by any one who happens to be reminded of it. There is no place, however, where this day so richly deserves to be honored by a formal recognition as at Yale College, for his generous sympathy in the days of its poverty and weakness, and for a benefaction which was as unique for its noble disinterestedness as it has been valuable for its permanent usefulness.

These are the reasons which have induced me to undertake the task of sketching the personal history of his romantic life, and of estimating the import and value of his services to philosophy and the Christian faith; remembering that to us he was a generous benefactor, who is none the less deserving of our affectionate honor, because of his goodness as a man, his genius as a philosopher, and his devotion as a Christian missionary.

Berkeley was born in Ireland near Thomastown, in the county of Kilkenny, of parents of English descent, and of respectable position and estate. He received his early classical education from the age of eleven to fifteen at the Duke of Ormond's school in Kilkenny, then called the Eton of Ireland. At fifteen he was matriculated at Trinity College in Dublin, the year before that in which Yale College was founded. Here he resided as student and fellow for thirteen years. Trinity College had from its reopening in 1592 been the one Protestant university of Ireland; sharing with the Protestant Establishment the weakness and limitations of its isolation, but now and then showing an enthusiasm and independence of its own such as was natural to its very position and the race which it educated. It has been called, with a slight suggestion of reproach, *the Silent Sister*, and yet it has now and then made its voice heard in a manner not altogether agreeable to its more decorous elders on the other side of the channel. At the time when Berkeley was a resident it was controlled by men of distinguished ability and marked independence. Its Provost for nearly all this time was the celebrated Peter Browne, afterwards Bishop of Cork, the author of two works, much talked of in their day; viz., "The Procedure, Extent, and Limits of the Human Understanding," 1728, and "Divine Analogy," 1733. William King became Archbishop of Dublin in 1703, and was author of the work on "The Origin of Evil," which was sharply criticized by Leibnitz and Bayle; and of some other notable theological treatises. Both these writers were foremost in the controversies of their own times. Their reputation has been recently revived by Whately,* Hamilton, Mansel,* and Herbert Spencer, all leaders in the modern speculations concerning agnosticism. Even the physics and metaphysics of Descartes were still under discussion. The new physics of Newton and the founders of the Royal Society were fighting their way into acceptance at Oxford. The new metaphysics of John Locke had recently begun to attract attention, his great work having been published only ten years when Berkeley began his studies at Dublin. Indeed, his college life was altogether a fermenting period for thought and action. To

* "Of the Right Method of Interpreting Scripture in what relates to the Nature of the Deity and his Dealings with Mankind," illustrated in a Discourse on Predestination, by Dr. King, late Lord Archbishop of Dublin, preached at Christ Church, Dublin, before the House of Lords; with notes by the Rev. Richard Whately, M. A., Fellow of Oriel College, Oxford. Oxford, 1821. Also, "The Limits of Religious Thought Examined," by Henry Longueville Mansel. London, 1858. Boston (reprinted), 1859.

hold a principle in philosophy, or politics, or religion was a serious business, when two or three claimants for the crown of England were ready to convulse the country with civil war. Ireland was still restless and unsubdued, having recently experienced a bloody rising and a bloody defeat. The sphere of speculation and of faith was beginning to be stirred in England and on the continent, by that materialistic and anti-Christian movement, which continued with occasional reactions till the bloody horrors of the French Revolution. It was altogether an exciting and uncertain period, especially for an ardent Irish youth at a Protestant University in Dublin, standing over against the Dublin Castle.

To all these exciting agencies Berkeley responded with the enthusiasm and energy of an ardent and self-relying spirit. "Ordinary people did not understand him and laughed at him. Soon after his entrance he began to attract attention as either the greatest genius or the greatest dunce in college." "He prosecuted his studies with simplicity and enthusiasm."

Early in 1705, when he was twenty years old, he formed a society with a few friends to promote and criticize the new philosophy of Boyle, Newton, and Locke. A well-filled and motley commonplace book still survives, abounding in every variety of suggestions in regard to the opinions which were discussed by his associates and himself, which indicates extraordinary breadth of inquiry and maturity of thought for a young man of from twenty to twenty-five years. We find in one place the recognition of a special call to himself of duty and of God to independent and bold speculation, and the expression of a sturdy resolve to be true to all his convictions. In other places, in brief jottings, we find many of the seeds of thought which took form and life in his subsequent treatises. His abundant references to all the recent writers in philosophy, mathematics, and physics show that he was fully abreast with his time.

In 1709, when he was twenty-four years old, he published his "Essay on a New Theory of Vision," which made an epoch in the analysis of the sense perceptions, and would of itself have made him immortal. It passed to a second edition in a year, and for clearness of style and skill of presentation, and above all for its suggestions of profound philosophical truth, is as well worth reading now as when it was first written. Not that many of the facts and phenomena were not already familiar, nor that their importance had not been recognized. Men had always known that one of the senses could, to some extent, be used for another; that they could and did judge of distance, and size, and motion by the pictures which the light paints on the eye; but they had never analyzed so skilfully, nor generalized so broadly, nor reasoned so convincingly as when Berkeley taught them that every act of vision is an act of judgment or interpretation, involving a rational process, more rapid indeed than what men call thinking, but an act of thought none the less.

The success of this essay was not owing to the facts which were first brought to light, for many of these had been known before, nor to the generalization which was derived from them that acts of vision are acts of interpretation, so that we see with the mind as truly as with the eyes, but to the clearness and felicity with which these facts are stated, and the convincing energy with which the several conclusions leap forth from the facts, all of which indicate philosophic genius. Berkeley did not write this essay simply as an analysis of sense perception. He had a higher aim than this. He would explode the received ideas of matter and force, and thus compel his readers by the analysis of the processes of vision to see and recognize the presence and agency of the living and the ever-present God. That this was his aim is evident from the outlines of an argument to this effect which we find in his commonplace book. This argument was resumed and partially completed in a treatise, published in 1710, when he was twenty-five years old, and entitled "A Treatise on the Principles of Human Knowledge." This was followed in 1713 by "Dialogues between Hylas and Philonous," in which the argument is carried to its conclusion. These three treatises set in motion a train of speculation which has never ceased to move till the present hour, the course of which can be traced through the skeptical and one-sided philosophies of England, Scotland, and France, and the idealistic and imaginative systems of Germany.

The doctrines of these three treatises of Berkeley's struck the world at first simply as paradoxes. But the sense of strangeness aroused and compelled sober inquiry. Inquiry not infrequently settled into conviction that God is nearer to man than man had supposed, even in the ordinary processes which seem to shut him out of sight. These give a deeper and truer meaning to the words, "who coverest thyself with light as with a garment," inasmuch as the analysis of vision reveals the truth that man, in interpreting the indications of color and outline, is compelled to assume the presence and agency of the Supreme Reason.* Berkeley's argument was, briefly, thus: The direct object of the mind's knowledge by any single act of sense can only be an affection of the mind, whether this object be a sight, a touch, or a sound.

* See Note A.

The product of two such acts conjoined can only be two of these together. Five can only give five conjoined—these five and nothing more. It follows that what we call matter or material objects are combinations or aggregates of sights and touches and smells, as perceived by, and, therefore, as affections of the mind. They are to us just what they are perceived to be, and they are perceived to be what they are felt to be —this, and nothing more. The material world in which each man lives, and which seems to him so solid and so real, is only his own world of possible and actual sensations. If he is blind, his world is a world of touches, smells, sounds, and tastes. If he is color-blind, two or three dingy colors constitute his visible universe. What we call the material world is what the senses give us, one by one, and all as their sum. When the swan floats gracefully on the surface of the mirroring lake, the perfectly reflected image that seems its other self is just as truly a visible reality as the floating figure which we can also touch and handle. The gorgeous rainbow, such as we sometimes see in the Adirondacks, that from the deep valley spans the mountain from three to five thousand feet upwards, is as truly real while it continues as are the everlasting hills on which are imprinted its fiery bars. The being of the sense world is its being perceived. *Esse est percipi.* There is no sense reality except what is thus experienced by the mind. What we know more and beyond is the constant connection of one sense object with another, or the absence of one when another is present. The swan which we can touch and see we call real. The swan that floats to the eye beneath the surface, but which we cannot find with the hand, we call unreal; and yet the one is as real to the eye as the other is to the hand. Hartley Coleridge, when five years old, did not answer to his name when called, but said, "Which Hartley is it? What, is there more than one? Yes, there is a deal of Hartleys. How so? There is picture Hartley, and shadow Hartley, and echo Hartley, and catch-me-fast Hartley."* "Which is the lying sense, feeling or seeing?" said Cheselden's blind boy just restored to sight, as he guessed with his eye and

* Poems and Memoir, Vol. I. page xxvii.

fumbled with his hands in the new and strange universe of vision that had just been new created for and by his unsealed eyesight.* But we do not rest contented with a single sense. We do not believe in the things outside till we learn to connect what we see with what we touch, and what we touch with what we see. But how do we learn to do this? Simply as we believe that we are in an honest universe,—a universe which is true in the signals or indicia which it presents for our confidence. For this belief our only security is in the reasonableness and truth of the one comprehensive mind that is ever acting upon our senses, and must be true to the signals which He gives. Hence we not only live and move and have our being in God, but we hear, and see, and touch by the signs to which He wakens our senses. Our own minds we know, because we use them. God we know by those combinations of sensations in which He is always present and true. Other minds we know through the occasional sense-combinations which we call their bodies. But God we always apprehend, because

* Phil. Trans., No. 402.

it is only as we believe in Him that we can connect a group of sensations into a material thing, one sensation with one or many as a cause or an effect, or interpret their presence or absence by fixed and rational laws. We shut our eyes, and the visible creation swims before our vision and seems about to sink into nothing; but as it seems to vanish, it is caught and held back by the ever-present thought and hand of God. We open them again, and the universe rises into a vision of beauty, as fresh and glowing when re-created by His fiat as when God for the first time said let there be light and there was light! To use Berkeley's own language, "Some truths there are, so near and obvious to the mind that a man need only open his eyes to see them. Such I take this important one to be,— to wit, that all the choir of heaven and furniture of the earth, in a word, all those bodies which comprise the mighty form of the world, have not any subsistence without the mind; that their being is to be perceived or known; that, consequently, so long as they are not actually perceived by me, or do not exist in my mind, or that of any other created spirit, they must either have no existence at all, or else subsist in the mind of some Eternal spirit."

"You, it seems, stare to find that God is not far away from every one of us, and that in Him we live and move and have our being; you, who, in the beginning of this morning's conference, thought it strange that God should leave himself without a witness, do now think it strange the witness should be so full and clear. *Alc.* I must own I do, * * * and never imagined it could be pretended that we saw God with our fleshly eyes as plain as we see any human person whatsoever, and that He daily speaks to our senses in a manifest and clear dialect. *Cri.* This language hath a necessary connection with knowledge, wisdom, and goodness; it is equivalent to a constant creation, betokening an immediate act of power and providence; it cannot be accounted for by mechanical principles, by atoms, attractions, or effluvia. The instantaneous production and reproduction of so many signs combined, dissolved, transposed, diversified, and adapted to such an endless variety of purposes, ever shifting with the occasions and suited to them, being utterly inexplicable and unaccountable by the laws of motion, by chance, by fate, or the like blind principles, doth set forth and testify the immediate operation of a spirit or thinking being; and not merely of a spirit which every motion or gravitation may possibly infer, but of one wise, good, and provident spirit which directs and rules and governs the world." *Alc. Dial.* IV., xiv.

This, in brief, is the Theistic Idealism with which Berkeley startled the world at the age of 25. Paradoxical as it seemed, it was expounded with singular clearness, illustrated with minute detail, defended with youthful ardor, and enforced with religious fervor. It is not at all surprising that it attracted immediate attention to its author, and made a place for him in every circle, if only as an object of wonder. It was, however, more easy to wonder and stare at him than it was to answer or silence him.

The facts on which Berkeley builds had been familiar for centuries, having started many a curious or skeptical inquiry.* But in almost every case the expounder had treated them in such a fashion as either to entangle his reader

---

* *Cf.* Malebranche, Rech. de la Vérité, I. ch. 9; Glanville, Scepsis Scientifica, ch. 5; Molyneux, Dioptrics; Locke's Essay, 4th ed. ch. ix. §8.

in a maze of refined distinctions, or bewilder him with a brilliant show of dazzling fireworks — silencing or bewildering, but not convincing him. Berkeley's statements, on the other hand, seem as clear as the sunlight and as solid as the pavement. He feels his way as cautiously as a blind man. He asks you if you are sure and steady at every step; and then, on a sudden, he turns upon you and asks where is the material universe. You look for it, and find that as a solid reality it is gone; and yet you are confident that you have destroyed or lost it by your own honest thinking. Your philosophic friend is so cool, so clear, so sure in every step, that you seem to have thought out every conclusion for yourself. At all events, you cannot lay your hand upon any single step and say it was false. The illusion is as when you look into a mountain lake whose margin is overlooked by a forest-clad mountain. You see every inch of its bottom as you peer over the edge of your floating boat. All is clear and sure, when in an instant the reflected mountain more than half displaces the oozy bottom, — a pictured show, indeed, in all its pomp of color and shadow, but so vivid that for an instant you cannot tell which is the reality and which the reflected image.

The effect of Berkeley's Idealism was no nine days' wonder. It became the problem of the century which followed; we should rather say it has continued to be the problem of nearly two centuries since. Hume took up what seemed to him a similar line of thought, and attempted to disintegrate the mind into a bundle of ideas, as Berkeley had sought to resolve matter into a series of impressions. Reid, who was roused by Hume's extremes to oppose both Hume and Berkeley, confesses to have been originally a convert to Berkeley's theory. Reid was followed in the direction of reaction by the learned and logical Hamilton. On the continent, sixty years after Berkeley composed his youthful Essay, Kant declares that he had been wakened by Hume and Berkeley from the dogmatic slumber in which he had been trained; and after Kant, and, as it would seem, by many growths and undergrowths, lo! this little sapling which our youthful friend planted in Dublin, has spread abroad into the great Banyan tree of Modern German Metaphysics, which has now struck its roots down from above, and then thrust its shoots up from beneath till its pillared shade has become a bewildering maze.* What is still more surprising is that the most distinguished men of the materialistic school in England at the present day, with rare exceptions, agree with Berkeley in resolving the material world into groups of sensations with "a permanent possibility of sensations," and the mind into "a series of feelings which is aware of itself as past and future." This is the painfully elaborated result of the life-long speculations of John Stuart Mill, who cannot be charged with any want of clearness, and whose system of Logic is a masterpiece of lucid statement and rigid consecution. Mill utterly repudiates Dr. Johnson's *argumentum baculinum* against Berkeley, but when he attempts to follow or correct him, he plunges us into a dim and misty cloud, without the play of that iridescent light

* See Note B.

which Berkeley sheds on every thought. Herbert Spencer and all the evolutionists resolve matter into sensations, and sensations into "nerve shocks" which are more complicated as they ascend into those higher potencies which men call matter and spirit or mind; but they find no God either within or behind these aspiring and ascending sensations. George H. Lewes and most of the positivists choose to resolve what they call phenomena into sensations, but make no provision, as does Berkeley, for a mind to originate or interpret nature or any agency which either uses or explains the scanty relationships by which they explain nature or justify either induction or evolution.*

I am not here to defend Berkeley's doctrine of Ideas. I am only desirous to defend him from being deemed a philosophical visionary for holding opinions which have been taught with more or less consistency by eminent individuals and famous schools. I am quite content to rest his defence on the unquestioned fact that he forced the philosophical world to grapple earnestly with

* See Note C.

his single problem for nearly two centuries, and that some of the most outspoken and positive of materialists of the present day are the most openly confessed of Berkeley's disciples as the outcome of all their physics and metaphysics.

While, then, our old and new fashioned materialists agree with Berkeley in resolving matter into sensations, and with Hume in resolving mind into feelings, they differ from Berkeley in one most important particular. That particular is that Berkeley's Idealism was characteristically Theistic. He was a Theist, not as a theologian or a Christian, but as a philosopher. He could not complete his theory of Ideas and find any order or trustworthiness in them, without God to produce and regulate them. If matter is nothing but ideas or sensations, still sensations require a spirit to feel or know them. If matter does not exist to produce them, there must be some agent to originate and sustain them, and that cause must be an eternal and all-embracing mind. Not only does he originate these ideas, but he must produce them in those combinations and in that order which justifies the common sense of experience and the theories of science. If every color we discern is an idea or impression produced in our minds by the agency of God, if every touch is the same, much more does the constant combination of every color with its appropriate touch, require his faithful care. According to Berkeley's theory, we need God to explain the one as truly as to explain the other. Without this faith in God we cannot even justify the experience of common life. Without this faith we cannot explain our confidence in the uniformity and stability of nature's operations. Without this faith we cannot justify our common sense and practical wisdom. Much less without it can we defend our faith in the theories or the experiments of science.

We may think as we will about Berkeley's theory of matter and of ideas, but as we listen to the bold challenge of his youth, that he intended to drive matter out of the universe that he might bring into it the living God, and trace the proof that all the conflicts which have followed have served to deepen the conviction that all true science supposes God to be a thinker and the student of science to be an interpreter of God's thoughts, we are disposed to honor his philosophical sagacity, as truly as to admire his intellectual courage.

If Berkeley did not drive matter out of the universe as effectually and as easily as he imagined he could, he certainly did bring in God as a permanent necessity for the satisfactory explanation of physical facts and their relations. As the result of all the controversies that have followed, so far as anything of this kind can be said to be settled, this is settled, that God, as self-existent reason and perhaps as rational love, must be assumed as the one fundamental axiom of scientific thought.

I have dwelt longer upon the history and real import of Berkeley's Idealism because it is often spoken slightingly of by those who look upon its superficial aspects, and know little or nothing of its place in the history of physical and metaphysical theories. Regarded by itself alone, even were it only a philosophical romance, it was a remarkable product not merely for a youth, but for a student of any age. But looked at in its place in the history of opinion, it is worthy of the highest honor. It is still more remarkable for its capacity to stimulate and sustain inquiry, especially when we trace its fermenting and stimulating power through the great philosophical revolutions of the last two centuries.

I may not omit to notice another significant passage in the history of Berkeley's university life,—his celebrated Sermons on Passive Obedience, which attracted some attention in those excitable times, and had more or less influence on his political fortunes. In these sermons he maintains the doctrine that an existing or established civil government may never be lawfully resisted or overthrown. He defended this position, not on the ground of divine or hereditary authority or right, but on strictly ethical principles, contending that no individual or party can ever be sure that the evils incident to a political revolution will not be greater than those involved in the continuance of a government, however bad may be its administration. This was another instance of his personal and logical boldness, as it is another exemplification of his clearness of thought and diction. It gave him additional notoriety just at the time when he left the life of a scholar and became more or less a man of the world, in times of political excitement and of general venality and corruption. For thirteen consecutive years previous to this he had resided at the university, and received all the degrees and perquisites to which he might properly aspire. For eight years afterwards, this connection was maintained, with renewed permissions of absence, and he lived more or less the life of a man of the world. First he visits London and is presented at court, making the acquaintance of the ministers of state, the bishops, the leading writers, as Addison, Steele, Pope, and Bolingbroke, apparently under the special direction of Dean Swift, his patron and friend. He seems everywhere to have been looked upon with wondering curiosity as a propounder of paradoxes that could not easily be answered, and yet he everywhere wins his way as one of the most delightful of companions and the best of men. He is stared at, and almost feared for his strange notions, and is as universally loved for his charming ardor, simplicity, and wit. The stately Atterbury, when asked by his relative, Lord Berkeley, what he thought of his kinsman at their first interview, replied: "So much understanding, so much knowledge, so much innocence, and such humility, I did not think had been the portion of angels till I saw this gentleman." Pope's well-known lines, written long after, when he had become a bishop, express the same enthusiastic admiration, which is the more significant because of its cynical accompaniments:

> Even in a bishop I can spy desert.
> Secker is decent; Rundel has a heart.
> Manners with candor are to Benson given.
> To Berkeley, *every virtue under heaven.*

The most of these eight years of wandering and uncertain life were spent on the continent; first, as a chaplain to the Earl of Peterborough in Italy, and, subsequently, as tutor and companion to pupils and friends. The letters and journals preserved from this period are brilliant and instructive. They indicate quick wit, high culture, and varied knowledge, combined with sincere and fervent religious feeling; a combination of excellencies not so common then as since.

On Berkeley's return to England in 1720, he found the kingdom in a condition of turmoil and almost despair, consequent on the explosion of the South Sea Scheme. His ardent soul, his quick wit and intense moral convictions found utterance in a paper entitled "An Essay towards preventing the Ruin of Great Britain," which is at once simple, thoughtful, keen, and Christian,— abounding in practical suggestions concerning the increase of national wealth, the care of the poor, the maintenance of roads, the introduction of manufactures, the fostering of art; coupled with fervid denunciations of gambling, licentiousness, and the neglect of religion among the higher classes. None but a bold and ardent soul like his could venture to address his fellow-countrymen in words so simple and so strong, and expect to be listened to. None but a man profoundly religious could utter words so biting in a spirit of gentleness and fervor. This Essay is of the utmost significance, as explaining the subsequent movements of his life and especially his mission to America.

Not long after his return to England, in the year 1721, he was made chaplain to the Lord-Lieutenant of Ireland; the year following he was made dean of Dromore, having previously been Senior Fellow of his University, and lecturer in Hebrew and Greek. In 1723 he met with a singular piece of good fortune, which deserves to be noticed as explaining in part the execution of his plans with respect to America. Miss Esther Van Homrigh, the Vanessa of Dean Swift's unhappy fate and memory, happened to meet Berkeley for once only at her mother's house, perhaps accompanied by the Dean, her unlucky and, as some would say, her faithless lover. This was not long, as it would seem, before the confession which she extorted from the latter, that he had already been secretly married to Stella. She was so chagrined at this intelligence, and so alienated from the Dean, that she at once destroyed the will in which she had constituted Swift her sole heir, and gave half her estate, some three thousand pounds and more, to Berkeley, the acquaintance of an hour. This was in 1723. In 1724 he was presented to the deanery of Derry, with an income of eleven hundred pounds, and found himself, for the first time in his life, in easy if not in affluent circumstances. And yet, in the same summer, we find him posting to London with a letter from Swift to the Lord-Lieutenant, in which he writes of Berkeley, after a humorous introduction: "He is an absolute philosopher with regard to money, titles, and power, and for three years past has been struck with a notion of founding a college at the Bermudas with a charter from the Crown. He has seduced several of the hopefullest young clergymen and others here, many of them well provided for, and all in the fairest way for preferment, but in England his conquests are greater, and I doubt will spread very far this winter. He showed me a little tract which he designs to publish; and there you will see his whole scheme of a life academic, philosophical —of a college founded for Indian scholars and missionaries; where he exorbitantly proposes

a whole hundred pounds a year for himself, fifty pounds for a fellow, and ten for a student. His heart will break if his deanery be not taken from him and left to your Excellency's disposal."
* * * "And, therefore, I entreat your Excellency to use such persuasions as will keep one of the first men of this kingdom at home, or assist him by your credit to compass his romantic design."

It would seem that this missionary project, or something like it, had been in his mind ever since his return to England from the continent, and the shock which he had received from the South Sea explosion with the revelations which it had given of the individual and social corruption in the Old World in respect to manners and morals and faith. From this scene, which excited only disgust and despair, he turned to the New World with ardent and enthusiastic hope. His well-known lines, though evincing little poetic genius, are the sober expression of his enthusiastic aspirations and his hopeful faith. They are at once a poem and prophecy, and they have made his name a household word from the Atlantic to the Pacific coast.

> The Muse, disgusted at an age and clime,
> Barren of every glorious theme;
> In distant lands now waits a better time,
> Producing subjects worthy fame.
>
> * * * * * * *
>
> There shall be sung another golden age,
> The rise of empires and of arts,
> The good and great inspiring epic rage,
> The wisest heads and noblest hearts.
>
> Not such as Europe breeds in her decay,
> Such as she bred when fresh and young,
> When heavenly flame did animate her clay,
> By future poets shall be sung.
>
> *Westward the course of empire takes its way,*
> The four first acts already past,
> A fifth shall close the drama with the day,
> Time's noblest offspring is the last.

His accession to a large income only kindled his zeal and inspired his courage for his new plan. "Yesterday," he writes, "I received my patent for the best deanery in the kingdom, that of Derry. It is said to be worth £1500 per annum, but I do not consider it with a view to enriching myself, and shall be perfectly contented if it facilitates and recommends my scheme of Bermuda." Again, earlier, he writes: "Here is something that will surprise your Lordship, as it doth me. Mrs. Hester Van Homrigh, a lady to whom I was a perfect stranger, having never in my life exchanged a word with her, died on Sunday night. Yesterday her will was opened, by which it appears that I am constituted executor, the advantage whereof is computed by those who understand her affairs to be worth £3000. * * * I know not what your thoughts are on the long account I sent you from London to Bath of my Bermuda scheme, which is now stronger on my mind than ever, this providential event having made many things easy in my private affairs, which were otherwise before."

The details of Berkeley's plan, the reasons for the selection of the Bermuda Islands, and the motives to the achievement are given at length in the tract entitled "A Proposal for the better Supplying of our Churches in our Foreign Plantations, and for Converting the Savage Americans to Christianity." It would seem that a general plan to this effect had long been seething in his mind, before the legacy of Miss Van Homrigh and his generous salary had placed him in a position to assume some responsibility and authority. The Bermuda Islands were for many years esteemed the most favorable location for his Christian college.

For three years after this plan had become a purpose he labored incessantly to interest in it men of political influence in church and state in and about London. Such was his zeal and skill, that he converted the most indifferent and obstinate into warm patrons and friends. Five thousand pounds were subscribed by private individuals. King George I. and his Prime Minister, Sir Robert Walpole, were committed to the project, and in 1725 a charter passed the seals, constituting the College of St. Paul's, with Berkeley at its head. In the year following, owing to Berkeley's pertinacity, twenty thousand pounds sterling were granted for the college out of certain lands sold in St. Christopher's Island, which promised to bring much more into the royal treasury. The distinctively missionary character of Berkeley's enterprise ought not to be overlooked, especially at a time when the opportunity and the obligation are understood and acknowledged as never before of propagating Christianity by means of institutions of Christian learning; and this both in the destitute portions of our own country and in those countries where Christianity is scarcely known as a faith or a spiritual power. That a man like Berkeley, who had been the favorite of courtiers and prelates and of royalty itself, who was admired and gazed at as the discoverer and defender of a new philosophy, fraught as he believed with the most important principles for Science and Faith, and was animated by the hope of fresh discoveries in the field of speculation, should have been moved by the impulse to plant a Christian university in a lonely and storm-vexed island and submit himself to narrow conditions of life for the spiritual welfare of the unruly colonists and the horrid savages, of which he had received such uninviting reports, and be able to kindle in others an enthusiasm similar to his own, is a singular phenomenon, even in the history of Christian devotion. That the disgust and despair which were excited by the contemplation of the rottenness of the old civilization and its effete Christianity should have elevated his faith and hope to the confidence of prophecy, invests his character and his mission with more than a romantic interest, while it exalts him to a high place in the roll of Christian Saints.

After many delays and disappointments, such as are incident to enterprises of this kind, in September, 1728, at the age of 43, having been recently married to a lady of kindred tastes and purposes, he embarked in a ship of 250 tons for Rhode Island, where the party landed after a voyage of little more than four months. The party consisted of the Dean and his wife, a lady friend, Miss Handcock, two gentlemen friends, John, afterwards Sir John

James, Bart., Mr. Richard Dalton, Mr. John Smybert, an artist of some promise, who was to be professor of architecture, painting, and drawing, and Mr. Peter Harrison, also an architect. Mr. Smybert and Mr. Harrison afterwards settled in Boston,— the first as a painter and architect, and the second as an architect. The first building in that city erected from Smybert's designs was the old State House; and the most noticeable building of Harrison's was the King's Chapel. Smybert's portraits are numerous and, aside from the interest which pertains to them as the earliest portraits painted in the country by a trained artist, are at least highly respectable for their time.

We are not informed why Berkeley did not sail directly for the Bermudas. It is, probably, that he thought it well not to commit himself to the establishment of his college till the royal promise was fulfilled. The reasons are manifold why he selected Rhode Island and Newport as the place of his temporary sojourn. Newport was then one of the most prosperous seaports on the entire Atlantic coast, with a free harbor, easy of access, and communicating readily with all the English islands and colonies, maintaining an active trade in all kinds of commodities, including negroes kidnapped in Africa. It was also a promising place for the advantageous investment in land of the funds of the college. It was a place of unlimited toleration for religious opinions, and a free port for the exchange of goods of all descriptions. The presence in this town of one or more missionaries at large of the Church of England was an additional attraction. Mr. Honeyman, the oldest, had been at Newport twenty-five years.* Trinity Church, in which he officiated, is still standing, with the organ which Berkeley gave to the parish. Across the bay, on the Narragansett peninsula, Dr. McSparran was the shepherd of a wealthy and rather unruly flock of Rhode Island planters, each one of

* History of the Episcopal Church in Narragansett, Rhode Island, etc., etc., by Wilkins Updike. New-York: Henry M. Onderdonk, 1847. The appendix contains "America Dissected," by Rev. Dr. McSparran, whose representations of the people of Connecticut are in striking contrast with those of Berkeley.

whom had his garret full of slaves and his stables full of Narragansett pacers,—who believed in good cheer and roystering hospitality quite as fervently as they did in the Church of England, to which the worthy Dr. held them by a somewhat doubtful tenure of spirituality. The free and fantastic *genius loci* even now seems to cast a bewildering glamour over the scenery of this entire region, and to infuse an exciting element into its very atmosphere. Such a fine nature as Berkeley's would respond to these influences, and also respond to the hereditary enthusiasm of the population for freedom and truth and spiritual activity. Indeed, Roger Williams and Berkeley are in many particulars kindred spirits. It is worthy of notice also that here and there was a little community of Friends, who were ready to respond to all that Berkeley could teach about the superiority of spirit to matter and the potency and purity of the spiritual life. It is not surprising that Berkeley found the air of Newport so sweet and exhilarating, and that his poetic eye rested upon its landscape with enthusiastic delight. It is worthy of notice, also, that there has never been a time since Berkeley blessed Rhode Island with his presence, when his theory has not been fervently held with poetic fervor, and ably defended with logical acuteness by some leading spirit among its citizens. Witness, Job Durfee, author of "*The Pan Idea,*" and Rowland G. Hazard, author of "*Man a Creative First Cause,*" etc., etc.

After residing in the town for some five or six months, he purchased an estate of ninety-six acres of land, which he called Whitehall, situated about three miles east from the harbor, on what is still known as Honeyman's Hill. It is altogether probable that he regarded this purchase as an investment, there being traditional testimony at least that his speculations were as enthusiastic in respect to the future value of real estate in that neighborhood as the most sanguine of dealers have as yet entertained. Here he erected the house which is still standing,— of moderate size and simple construction, but giving evidence of art and of taste. In form and material and workmanship, it is creditable to its owner and his architect, although it has suffered not a little from neglect and shabby additions. But the scenery can never be marred. It is the same now as when Berkeley's eye rested upon it and his pen described it, with the exception of the loss of many a surviving forest tree majestic in form and size, and many a shadowy wood setting off the beauty of slope and lawn, or breaking against the sky or ocean. There remain the alternations of its gentle and abrupt undulations, of its glimpses and stretches of bay and ocean, of the varied combinations of sand and rock and turf, the latter always green from fog and shower, and the breeze that ever attends the swell of the restless ocean. The scene is none the less attractive now than when it was once the delightful home of our philosopher, who loved nature with the heart of the poet and loved his kind with the enthusiasm of humanity, who found God in nature not more by the necessities of his philosophy, than by the cravings of his heart,—who, with the rarest symmetry, combined in himself the characteristics of philosopher, poet, and saint.

Having settled himself to the life of a country gentleman, he waited with whatever patience he could command till the £20,000 of which he had been assured by King and Parliament should be forwarded by the order of the Minister. But he did not give himself up to an inactive life. He cultivated the solid acres of his estate with as much earnestness as he had speculated to the conclusion that they were only tough and intractable ideas. He rejoiced in "the still air of delightful studies" which his temporary retreat enforced upon him. He preached now and then, and all classes of people flocked to hear his winning and temperate words. Not a few stubborn Quakers were seen among his hearers, though they would neither bend the knee nor lift their broad-brimmed hats. He instituted a philosophical society, the outcome of which still exists in the famous Redwood Library. The condition of the remnants of the Indian tribes and of the negroes who were held in slavery moved him to Christian pity, and he bemoans the unchristian neglect of their spiritual condition by their masters, and the denial to them of Christian baptism from certain logical or conscientious scruples. It is interesting to find in the record on the books of Trinity Church the following entry of baptism: "June 11, 1731. Philip Berkeley, Anthony Berkeley, Agnes Berkeley, negroes, received into the church."

Singularly enough, Berkeley appears never to have traveled in New England. He did not even go to Boston till he saw it on his return to England, though Smybert soon settled there. There were obvious reasons in the badness of the roads, and the absence of post-coaches, and the limitations of sloop navigation even to New-York and New Haven.

On the other hand, it was altogether natural and decorous that the few missionaries of the Church of England who were within his reach should be attracted to the presence of a dignitary so high as a dean. Conspicuous among them was Rev. Samuel Johnson, of Stratford, Conn., who was one of the tutors who in 1722 had, with the rector of Yale College, been led to question the validity of any other than Episcopal ordination, and with him and another tutor had resigned his office. In his visit to England for Episcopal orders, a few years before, he had become acquainted with and attracted by Berkeley's ideal philosophy, and could do no less than hasten to Newport and confer with its welcome visitant in respect to their common faith and common philosophy. The result of this and other visits was a warm personal friendship which extended to the families of both, and was continued for more than one generation. First the Rev'd, afterwards Dr., Johnson, and subsequently the President of Columbia College, he became a sturdy adherent of the Berkeleian system, and in 1752 published a book in its defence, which was printed by Dr. Franklin in Philadelphia. It is entitled *"Noetica, or Things relating to the Mind or Understanding, and Ethica, or Things relating to the Behavior."* It is able and original, and does credit to the breadth and acuteness of its author.

Johnson, as was natural, explained to his curious and intelligent listener all that he knew of the social and religious life of New England. By his influence, doubtless, Rector Williams, of Yale College, was brought into correspondence with the Dean. The influence of Rev. Jared Eliot of Killingworth, now Clinton, the friend of Dr. Franklin, one of the fellows of the college, was also put into requisition to interest Berkeley in the young institution. The evidence is ample that Johnson was kindly and generous in his charity towards the college which had educated him and of which he had been an officer. It appears from their correspondence that when Berkeley at first proposed to send a few books to the library he was doubtful whether they would be welcomed, on account of their bearing upon the question of church-polity. And yet from all that this frank correspondence reveals, the attitude of both these gentlemen to the college, which was then identified with the Congregational system, was singularly magnanimous. The result in the subsequent benefaction of Berkeley is a decisive proof that this must have been true of both. It was reported by one of his hearers that Berkeley had taken the pains to say in the pulpit, "Give the devil his due, John Calvin was a great man." All his utterances with respect to Puritan and Romanist prove that he was singularly broadminded in respect to all "who profess and call themselves Christians."

As we have already explained, Berkeley regarded himself as a mere sojourner in Rhode Island. Some suggestions or overtures must have been made to induce him to establish his college at Newport. But he declined them all, and adhered to his original determination. Here he waited, anxiously expecting favorable tidings from England of the dispatch of his long-expected twenty thousand pounds, and doubtless occasionally chafing under the unexplained delay. On one occasion this delay is excused by the fear started by the Court party, that the establishment of a missionary college in America might tend to the independency of the colonies. Under all these vexations his resolute and upright spirit continually appears in his letters. While he insists on the one hand that the money pledged by king and parliament would certainly be paid, and the more inasmuch as the Crown had already received three times this amount from the sales at St. Kitts, and while he confesses that except for his own pledge he would sooner be in Londonderry, of which he was dean, than to remain in Rhode Island, yet he declares that he shall remain in Rhode Island till the question is decided, even at the risk of losing his deanery and its ample salary. This suspense was finally terminated. The bishop of London presses Walpole for a decisive answer, and finally obtains it in the following very intelligible terms: "If you put the question to me as a minister, I must and can answer you that the money shall undoubtedly be paid, as soon as suits the public convenience; but if you ask me as a friend whether Dean Berkeley shall continue in America, expecting the payment of twenty thousand pounds, I advise him by all means to return to Europe and give up his present expectations."

This answer Berkeley regarded as decisive, and in the autumn of 1731 he sailed for London, having spent about three years in America.

True to his cause, and with no abatement of love or zeal, he preaches, soon after his landing, the annual sermon before the venerable Society for the Propagation of the Gospel, in which he re-expresses his old convictions in respect to the obligation to found seminaries of Christian learning in the colonies, at the same time that he manifests the most catholic feeling and just appreciation of the value and usefulness of the colleges and "religious societies" which he had found in America. The interest already felt in Yale College, which had been fostered by the magnanimous devotion of Dr. Johnson, was again manifested by the conveyance to it of his estate of ninety-six acres in Rhode Island, as the foundation of the Berkeley scholarships. If we consider the circumstances under which this gift was offered, and the condition of the college at the time it was made, it was one of the most generous gifts which it ever received. If we also consider the man by whom it was given and the circumstances under which it was offered, it is one of the most worthy to be commemorated. The income of this estate was set apart to provide three Berkeley scholarships for the promotion of classical learning.* These scholarships have been proposed every year till the present, although the income which they bring of fifty-five dollars a year is not very stimulating. To be a Berkeley scholar was formerly a distinguished honor, and it is greatly to be regretted that, in consequence of the foundation of more lucrative fellowships, these prizes are now not more earnestly sought for. No more desirable gift in the interests of classical learning, in Yale College, can be named, than the enlarged endowment of these three scholarships into classical fellowships worthy of the name of Berkeley. In the year 1733 Berkeley made another princely gift to the library from himself and his friends of about one thousand volumes, valued at four hundred pounds, many of which still remain in good condition, and stand as a perpetual memorial of the munificent generosity of our great benefactor. A similar gift was also sent to Harvard College, which was unfortunately destroyed by fire in 1764.

* See Note E.

But I have not done with Berkeley's life in America, nor with the fruits which it bore. The greatest and most memorable achievement of his residence in America is his work called "Alciphron, or the Minute Philosopher." This was composed at Whitehall, much of it beneath the well-known Hanging Rocks near his own home, and contains abundant references to the scenery by which he was surrounded and the life which he lived. For acuteness of logic, for convincingness of argumentation, for felicity of illustration, for elevation of sentiment, and for marvellous clearness and purity of style, this work is justly distinguished as a classical treatise in English philosophical literature. It is not extravagant to say that it is the best reproduction of the Platonic Dialogue which we have in the English language. It abounds in local color and allusions. One who stands on Honeyman's Hill and turns over its pages, can follow with his eye the several features of the landscape which the author wrought into his pictures of nature and of life. Even a group of fox-hunters rushes across the landscape as Berkeley had seen them many a time in Narragansett. One almost feels the Newport breezes as he re-creates the visions which the author depicts. From every page the reader has fresh impressions of the exhilarating yet placid life which this saintly enthusiast was living in the New World, while he was waiting impatiently to labor for its good. It is of little consequence how we decide the question whether this treatise should be classed among the products of English or American literature, so long as it is breezy with the American atmosphere and bright with American life.

The theme, however, was in no sense American. The movement which it described and sought to resist was English, as the writers and thinkers who are portrayed and criticized are English as seen at a distance by a looker-on, through the loopholes of his remote retreat. Viewed dogmatically, it was a portraiture and criticism of the negative opinions of the times. It was an honest attempt to arrest the tide of atheistic and anti-Christian opinion, then at its flood, which had been flowing for a half-century, and which ebbed at last in the bloody ooze and foam of the French Revolution. This unbelief was Protean in its phases, from the pot-house ribaldry of Mandeville to the ambitious Platonism of Shaftesbury, from the daring acuteness of Collins to the subtle insinuations of Hume. Its pervasive energy was more complete over both the cultivated and the common mind than ever before or since. The contest between faith and unbelief was severe, and the issue at times seemed doubtful. Notwithstanding the solid and varied ability of the learned champions of Theistic and Christian Truth, and the fiery and fervent zeal of the Great Evangelistic Revival, which arrested its course, it was not till Europe had seen and felt the judgments of God, near the close of the last century, that the reaction was complete in both faith and morals, in literature and public sentiment. The writings on both sides of this controversy are a library themselves, and the most of them now repose in ponderous dignity upon dusty shelves; but among them there are two of conspicuous value, and these are the "Analogy" of Butler and the "Alciphron" of Berkeley, the one of which was published in 1736, and the other in 1732.

The value of Berkeley's treatise for the modern reader is not alone or chiefly in its arguments, cogent and keenly put as most of them are. It lies rather in its lifelike and piquant pictures of the times, and the keen and genial humor with which the author disposes of the crowd of freethinkers as they pass in review before him, holding up their motley creeds and their thin and shabby philosophies of life. As a picture of the times, "Alciphron" is of priceless and permanent value. It can never be antiquated so long as philosophy shall renew its foolish and never-ending battle with personality in man and in God, or criticism shall back its new theories with the old assumption that there is no God in history, or that He cannot break the methods of nature when man needs to be confronted with His personal presence. The reader of "Alciphron" will find that Agnosticism is no novelty as a philosophical theory, although in Berkeley's day it was propounded on the one hand by a provost and a bishop, and on the other by troops of indolent doubters, similarly as in our time it has been taught by an Oxford divine on the one hand, and on the other by a philosopher who claims to be master in every line of thinking. Dr. Dwight in the year 1803 procured the republication of this treatise as an antidote to the infidelity of his times. It was printed in New Haven, and stray copies are to be found in some of the old houses in Connecticut. I ought not to omit to mention that the work first appeared in England in March, 1732, two months after Berkeley arrived in London, and that it passed to a second edition the same year. I am also reminded that I ought to say a word of Berkeley as a writer of English prose, inasmuch as he is, perhaps, at his best in "Alciphron." His acquaintance with Dean Swift in Dublin and with Richard Steele in London, as also a multitude of incidents besides, show very clearly that he sympathized warmly with the critical and other influences which produced the English style of Queen Anne. Not long after his first emergence in London, we find him contributing several papers, fourteen in all, to the *Guardian*, from the 14th of March to the 5th of August, several of which are *quasi* satirical and argumentative against the freethinkers. All of these are marked by the lively combination of wit and argument which distinguish his maturer works. While they are not inferior to the essays by his associates, they are not specially distinguished by the simplicity, smoothness, and freedom on the one hand, and the crispness, brevity, and personal flavor on the other, which distinguish his more elaborate works. Of the style of all these writings, hardly any praise can be too extravagant. The wordiness and mannerism which make the essays of Addison to drag somewhat heavily are absent from all the disquisitions of Berkeley; while the personality of the author finds full and forcible expression in the easy use of a diction which fits his thoughts like a well-made garment. Not unfrequently a colloquial term or epithet is allowed, but never with any loss of dignity or sacrifice of strength; while good-natured humor gives a fresh and spicy flavor to the strong and vigorous thoughts which are never wanting.

Berkeley had returned to England somewhat weakened in health but unbroken in spirits, with his energy and ardor not a whit abated. He seems to have lingered awhile among his many friends in and about London, and to have renewed his attendance at Court and his philosophical interviews with the metaphysical Queen Caroline, the pupil of Leibnitz and the patron of Bishop Butler. He must have had some promise of preferment, as in 1734 he was made Bishop of Cloyne, in Ireland, a diocese not far from Cork. He settled himself at once in this attractive home, and devoted all his energies to his official duties and the interests of the people of Ireland. He very soon published the "Analyst," which occasioned not a little excitement among the mathematicians. In it he resumed a line of argument which he had suggested years before, that the higher mathematics employed conceptions which involved assumptions which as truly exclude rational definitions as do any of the mysteries of the Christian faith. This was followed by a war of pamphlets, and excited not a little asperity of feeling. Some years after, he began the publication of the "Querist," which was issued in three parts, and contained in all about six hundred brief and telling questions respecting the disabilities of Ireland, many of which involve the profoundest principles of political and social science. The doughty and dogmatic Warburton writes of it in 1750 as "well worth attending to by the Irish nation. He is indeed a great man, and the only visionary that I ever knew that was." *(Letters, etc.)* Sir James Mackintosh says: "Perhaps the 'Querist' contains more hints, then original, still unapplied, in legislation and political economy, than are to be found in any equal space." Many of these hints sparkle with humor, and they are all inspired with humane and patriotic feeling, in which the ecclesiastic and the humorist are lost sight of in the Christian and the man. Had the half of these suggestions been followed at the time they were made, the subsequent history of Ireland, and of England in its relations to Ireland, would have been in far less measure a history of tears and of blood.

Berkeley resided in Cloyne about eighteen years, during much of which time he was occupied with a singular subject of practical and speculative interest. This was none other than the virtues of *Tar-water* for the cure of a great variety of bodily diseases, which he was led oddly enough to connect with the highest themes of human speculation. As the result of his experiments and speculations, he published in 1744 an essay which in its second edition was called "Siris," a chain of philosophical reflections and inquiries concerning the virtues of tar-water and divers other subjects which he contrived to connect together and attach to his singular theme. This book, he used to say, cost him more thought and research than any other of his life. It was wittily and truly said of it that it began with tar-water and ended with the Trinity. Whatever might be said of its metaphysical value, it cannot be questioned that it was first inspired by a truly humane interest. Not long after Berkeley's removal to Cloyne, the whole country was desolated by famine and epidemic dysentery. The Bishop remembered that, when in Rhode Island, he had heard of resin, turpentine, and tar as favorite remedies for diseases of this kind, especially with the Indians, and had been induced to make a trial of their virtues. He found the remedy so efficacious that he recommended it in letters to his friends, and then more publicly, as might be expected. It was not long before he found himself the champion and patron of the remedy in which his confidence had so rapidly increased. The members of the medical profession were irate at the intermeddling of a layman in matters of bodily healing, even though he was so revered an ecclesiastic in matters spiritual; while the Bishop's zeal and pertinacity were enforced by his human sympathy, in spite of the opposition and ridicule of the Faculty. Manufactories of tar-water were set up in England and America, and "Siris" was translated into several of the European languages.

The excitement and the humor of the situation are well set forth in the following lines by the Bishop:

To drink or not to drink, that is the doubt;
With pro or con the learned would make it out.
Britons, drink, the jolly prelate cries;
What the prelate persuades, the doctor denies.
But why need the parties so learnedly fight?
A choleric Jurin so fiercely indite?
Since our senses can tell if this liquor be right.
What agrees with his stomach and what with his head,
The drinker may feel though he can't write or read.
Then authority is nothing, the doctors are men,
And who drinks tar-water will drink it again.

That the remedy should prove so popular is not surprising to one who remembers that various preparations of tar are still sold as sovereign remedies for manifold diseases. I do not propose to trace the links of the chain by which Berkeley connects the resinous element in tar with the highest flights of human speculation. To do so would require an analysis of the chemistry and physiology and physics of Berkeley's time, which were crude enough at the best. The logic of Berkeley's attempt may remind us of sundry speculations in our own times in respect to ozone, with its fancied relations to resin and tar and its supposed life-giving and life-renovating qualities. A still better modern instance in the opinion of some might be furnished by the aspiring speculations by which such a thinker as Professor Clifford found *mind-stuff* in every earthy substance with the capacity of being transformed into spirit under the requisite scientific conditions, or in the confidence with which Professor Huxley makes dead matter lift itself up into living protoplasm, or the sanguine Tyndall sees visions of rudimentary philosophers floating in fiery clouds, or Herbert Spencer evolves the universe of living spirits out of the original fire-mist by the impulse acquired in its first rush "from a rarer to a denser medium." There is this difference in favor of Berkeley's theory, that the Absolute which he finds or assumes, when he is reached, is intelligent, personal, and supreme. The new metaphysics of materialistic evolution has provided for its thinkers a ladder by which men seem to ascend to the loftiest heights of speculation without finding either angels or God; and for this reason, if for no other, it is hardly fair to sneer at Bishop Berkeley for seeking to trace the steps by which ancient speculation sought to ascend upward to the ineffable and the absolute, and to connect matter and spirit and God by the attenuated links of the subtle chain which binds being and thought together.

John Stuart Mill thinks that while Siris adds nothing "of the smallest value to Berkeley's thoughts elsewhere expressed, it overloads them with a heap of useless and mostly unintelligible jargon, not of his own, but of the Plotinists." Professor Fraser, his eminent biographer, as also his zealous critic and disciple, finds in it a restatement in the terms of the ancient schools of his original idealism, with important modifications of the thoughts which in his earlier writings are so sharply cut and clearly enounced.

To us it seems to be rather a collection of the speculations of the old philosophers and the current physicists on the elements and products which make up the universe of matter and spirit;—and these rather as materials for meditation than as teaching, or even suggesting a completed system. It is the work of a philosopher, poet, and divine, composed as he might be supposed to sit in his well-furnished library while he glances at the titles of the folios that stand upon the shelves, till he finds himself thinking aloud while he meditates on their opinions on one subject or another, after the subtle logic of a memory that had at once been enriched and stimulated by the studies of half a century; with his hand always upon Plato, his favorite author, as he is represented in his portrait. Doubtless, the threads of connection are now and then peculiar to himself, but in general they are easy to be followed, even though they are not in the line of the severest logic. Many of these thoughts are profound for their practical wisdom, and breathe the spirit of noble enthusiasm. There are not a few passages of the most elevated sentiment, expressed in language which has made them classical. The following are

not infrequently quoted and referred to, but can never be pondered too seriously:

"Prevailing studies are of no small consequence to a state, the religion, manners, and civil government of a country, ever taking some bias from its philosophy, which affects not only the minds of its professors and students, but also the opinions of all the better sort, and the practice of the whole people, remotely and consequently, indeed, though not inconsiderably. Have not the polemic and scholastic philosophy been observed to produce controversies in law and religion? And have not fatalism and Sadducism gained ground, during the general passion for the *Corpuscularian* and mechanical philosophy, which hath prevailed for about a century. * * * Certainly had the philosophy of Socrates and Pythagoras prevailed in this age, among those who think themselves too wise to receive the dictates of the Gospel, we should not have seen interest take so fast hold on the minds of men, nor public spirit to be γενναίαν εὐήθειαν a generous folly, among those who are reckoned to be the most knowing as well as the most getting part of mankind.

"It might well be thought serious trifling to tell my readers that the greatest men had ever a high esteem for Plato, whose writings are the touchstone of a hasty and shallow mind; whose philosophy has been the admiration of ages; which supplied patriots, magistrates, and law-givers to the most flourishing states, as well as fathers to the church and doctors to the schools. Albeit, in these days the depths of that old learning are rarely fathomed; and yet it were happy for these lands if our young nobility and gentry, instead of modern maxims, would imbibe the notions of the great men of antiquity. But in these freethinking times, many an empty head is shook at Aristotle and Plato as well as at the Holy Scriptures." (331.)

What can be finer than the conclusion:

"The eye by long use comes to see even in the darkest cavern! and there is no subject so obscure but we may discern some glimpse of truth by long poring on it. Truth is the cry of all, but the game of a few. * * * He that would make a real progress in knowledge must dedicate his age as well as his youth, the later growth as well as first fruits, at the altar of Truth." (368.)

The domestic life of Berkeley at Whitehall and at Cloyne was eminently elevated and lovely. He cherished the acts and amenities of culture, with ardent and sustained enthusiasm. Music, drawing, and painting were followed by many if not all of his household. A contemporary thus describes his home: "He has successfully transplanted the polite arts, which before flourished in a warmer soil, to this northern climate. Painting and music are no longer strangers in Ireland, or confined to Italy. In the Episcopal palace of Cloyne, the eye is entertained with a great variety of good paintings, as well as the ear with concerts of excellent music. There are here some pieces of the best masters, as a Magdalen of Rubens, some heads by Van Dyke and Kneller, besides several good paintings performed in the house, etc." He writes himself: "Your care in providing the Italian psalms set to music, the four-stringed bass violin, and the antique bass viol, requires our repeated thanks. We have already a bass viol made in Southwark 1730, and reputed the best in England, and through your means we are possessed of the best in France." His paternal love and tenderness are conspicuous in all his letters. Of his daughter he writes: "But such a daughter! so bright a little gem; that to prevent her doing mischief among the illiterate squires I am resolved to treat her like a boy and make her study eight hours a day." Of his favorite son who died: "I was a man relieved from the amusement of politics, visits, and what the world calls pleasure. I had a little friend educated always under my own eye, whose painting delighted me, whose music ravished me, and whose lively, gay spirit was a continual feast. It has pleased God to take him hence. God, I say, in His mercy hath deprived me of this pretty, gay plaything. His parts and person, his innocence and purity, his particular uncommon affection for me, had gained too much upon me. Not content to be fond of him, I became vain of him. I had my heart too much upon him, more perhaps than I ought to have done upon anything in this world." His wife was a person of attractive manners and many accomplishments, but especially distinguished for her saintly and so-called pietistic temper. An effective and brilliant portrait of her husband from her hands is at Trinity College, Dublin.

It is pleasant to know that during the twenty years or more of Berkeley's life after leaving

America, he maintained an intimate friendly intercourse with the Johnson family, and that he expressed his continued gratification at the prosperity of this college till the end of his life, as also at the spirit in which his benefaction was regarded and administered. In 1745 he gave some excellent suggestions to Dr. Johnson respecting the foundation of King's, since Columbia, College, of which the Doctor was the first president, and uniformly expressed entire satisfaction in the results of his own efforts to promote Christian education in this country.

It will be remembered that it accorded with his tastes, and was a feature of his plan to provide in his college not only appliances for instruction in the classics, mathematics, and theology, but also for culture in the fine arts, especially in music, drawing, painting, and architecture. He brought with him, as his professor of drawing, painting, and architecture, John Smybert, then a painter in London who had made good studies in Italy. Before the scheme of the college was abandoned, Smybert established himself in Boston, where he was the first portrait painter of any reputation which Boston had known.

We have already noted that as an architect Smybert furnished the designs for the old State House in that city, which is still carefully preserved. Peter Harrison was an architect by profession, a pupil of Sir John Van Brugh, who, after a sojourn in England, returned to Boston for the remainder of his life. He gave the designs for the present King's Chapel in 1749, which alone should invest his name and memory with respect.

With his two other companions Berkeley maintained an intimate and unbroken friendship till the end of his own life. Mr. Dalton survived him. Mr., afterwards Sir, John James became a member of the Roman Catholic communion in 1741, not long before his death. His intention to do this called forth a long letter from Berkeley, in which his conceptions of the Christian life and the evidences of the Christian system are set forth at great length and with a delightful catholicity of spirit towards all Christian believers. It is interesting to know that

Sir John had announced his intention to give the Bishop the bulk of his large fortune, but was dissuaded by what is called a "thundering letter" from Berkeley to Dalton, saying: "Do you tell James that I will not have his fortune."

In 1752 Berkeley carried into effect a plan which he long had in mind, viz., to resign his Episcopate, that he might superintend the education of his second surviving son and enjoy complete retirement from active service. His petition to be allowed to resign was presented to the King, who replied that "he should die as bishop, but might live where he pleased." Accordingly, he went to Oxford to live a retired life, but survived only a few months. On the evening of the 14th of January, 1753, while his wife was reading from the fifteenth chapter of the First Epistle to the Corinthians, his daughter turned to offer him a cup of tea, and found that he was gone from the earth.

There could scarcely be a more fitting death after a life of such eminent usefulness. A man so conspicuously unworldly, so acute in intellect, accomplished in culture, unselfish in spirit, joyous in his sympathy with art and science and learning, buoyant in spirit and serene in his Christian hopes, was fitly dismissed from the earth by an Ethanasian such as this.

Here ends my simple and I fear somewhat tedious narrative. It speaks for itself, and I trust will furnish all the apology which I need to make for attempting to commemorate the two-hundredth birthday of one whose connection with Yale College is one of the most interesting events in its annals. My esteemed predecessor, Rector Williams, in a letter of thanks to Berkeley, expresses the conviction that the college will be moved by a sense of gratitude to " always retain a favorable opinion of his idea of material substance as consisting in a stated union and combination of sensible ideas." No student of logic or philosophy will, it is hoped, be so obtuse as not to appreciate the sharp analysis and compact logic which led Berkeley to his idealism, or to esteem the work of criticism and reply to be easy. But whatever may be thought of his philosophy, we are confident that no man who becomes familiar with his character and follows his career can withhold from him the tribute of affectionate admiration.

In the chapel of our daily worship two windows always meet the eyes of the congregation — one honored with the name of Jonathan Edwards and the other with that of George Berkeley. Each was distinguished for acuteness of intellect, for vigor of logic, for Christian and missionary self-devotion, and for an ardent interest in Christian education. May these names ever be honored and the men who bore them; and as Yale College becomes more emphatically and conspicuously than now the home of Christian science and of Christian letters, may these names glow with a still brighter lustre in its annals.

APPENDIX.

NOTE A.—It is worthy of notice that only a few years afterwards, surrounded, as it were, by similar logical and spiritual impulses, Jonathan Edwards drew the same conclusions as Berkeley had done from the same data in Locke's Essay, which he studied in Yale College at the age of 14. Among his "Notes on the Mind"[*] there is to be found a complete and consistent system of idealism which is almost identical with Berkeley's. It has been conjectured that possibly at the time when these notes were written, between 1717 and 1719, Edwards may have seen a copy of one of Berkeley's earlier treatises, published from seven to nine years before; perhaps through the agency of Dr. Johnson, who was tutor in the college at that time. There is no evidence that a copy of any of the works referred to was known at the college, and there is reason to believe that they were not then accessible. Indeed, Dr. Johnson is said to have first become interested in Berkeley's idealism when he went to England in 1723 for Episcopal ordination. Edwards makes no reference to Berkeley, nor does he intimate that any writer had suggested the argument for idealism to his mind. The state-

[*] See Works of President Edwards. New-York, 1830. Vol. I., Note H., p. 664.

ments and reasonings are all apparently the honest and independent conclusions of his surpassingly clear and logical understanding. These notes, though the work of Edwards's youth between the ages of 14 and 18, it should be remembered were first printed in the year 1830.

In his treatise on Original Sin, Edwards employs phraseology that was distinctively Berkeleian, and uses language which indicates, without naming Berkeley, that he has him distinctly in mind. Some other New England theologians have employed definitions and processes of reasoning in which the idealism of Berkeley may be distinctly traced, if it is not distinctly confessed. To these they were doubtless impelled by the tendency of the Calvinistic theology to exalt the Deity in every relation which he can hold to man or the universe.

NOTE B.—The attention of most of the students and critics of modern speculation has more generally been limited to the idealism of Berkeley as the distinctive and salient feature of his teaching, which aroused the attention of his critics in unwearied efforts for its refutation; and in that way stimulated philosophic inquiry, and brought into existence comments, criticisms, and emendations without number, in all the Protean forms of modern speculation. Thus it is conceived that Hume followed Berkeley only with a wider and more consistent application of his critical questioning, simply by a stricter and more rigorous adherence to his method; that Stewart and Hamilton were aroused to protest against the premises and method of both by a *reductio ad absurdum;* while Kant, with a more searching analysis, tore away the imperfect foundations on which all had builded, and supplied their place with a structure of his own, which his successors in their turn have sought to destroy and replace.

The sole service that Berkeley is supposed to have rendered was to demonstrate the weakness of Locke's "Analysis" by a consistent application of some of his definitions, and a somewhat narrow and over-rigorous interpretation of his theory of the origin and nature of knowledge. Hence Locke, Berkeley, and Hume are more commonly grouped together as the consistent disciples of the same school,— with which the Scottish philosophers are supposed to have a very close connection, and against which the German school was aroused to an effective protest. The single peculiarity by which Berkeley is distinguished in the view of such critics is by his persistent idealism, *i. e.*, his denial of the reality of matter, which is regarded as somewhat less consistent and rigorous than Hume's denial of spirit; while both are held to be desperate Nihilists in respect to everything besides, that philosophy cares or contends for.

A close scrutiny of his system will reveal the truth, that Berkeley confined his negative or skeptical position to the denial of matter as an obscure, unknown something over and beyond the ideas occasioned or produced in the human mind; while in respect to every other important position he was far in advance of his time, and anticipated many of the questions with which modern speculation has been forced to concern itself, and most of the conclusions which the soundest philosophy accepts. As an idealist, he denied the metaphysical necessity of matter; but by the same necessity he affirmed the reality of spirit, not only as the agent or subject of the act of knowledge, but as the object of the same in the form of ideas. Spiritual being he held to be directly known as the conscious ego which is the agent of knowledge; as the free and responsible ego which is moral; and as the Eternal spirit who wakens in dependent spirits those ideas of which the senses are capable, and binds them together in those relationships which make memory, experience, and science possible. Berkeley was eminently a Theistic idealist, affirming the necessary and self-evident existence of the absolute Spirit as the permanent sustainer of those ideas which alternately wake and sleep, die and live again, in the subjective experiences of those dependent spirits that have their being in Him. What was still more important in a philosophic sense, he affirmed the original capacity in the human spirit to discern and trust in *the relations of ideas by direct intuition;* which relations are the laws of God's actings in the objective universe of ideas, and the conditions of man's subjective interpretation of the same. In a word, his system provided for God, for created and dependent spirits, and for the permanent manifestation of God in ideas, connected by permanent relationships, which are interpretable by man, and thus form the **materials for** Science **and** Religion, and the media for a constant communication between God and man.*

It is true all these points of his system were not in his lifetime fully expanded or formally defended, for the reason that they were not fully appreciated by current criticism — neither as to what they displaced nor as to what they supplied. This is explained in great part by the circumstance that Locke had completely taken possession of the thinking of his times, **and been** accepted in the general judgment as having started all the problems and answered all the questions which could possibly be asked or thought of. The more **conspicuous** was this sagacity of Berkeley for this **very** reason, and the higher his claim to the eminence which is his rightful due. We venture the opinion that, as Berkeley becomes a second time the object of critical attention in the light of modern research, his reach of thought and his comprehensive sagacity

* *Cf.* Principles of Human Knowledge, 89.

will be more and more highly appreciated, and his name will rank higher in the estimation of philosophical critics and historians. It will be seen more and more clearly and be acknowledged more generally that he not only rendered an important service in his time by his earnest protest against serious oversights in current speculation, but that his direct contributions to the principles which philosophy must hold as fundamental were by no means inconsiderable. Most of these positions are announced rather than expanded; they are proposed rather than defended. Their varied and manifold applications, and their indispensable necessity to the interests of science and of faith, had not been brought to light by Kant's critical analysis. Notwithstanding all this, or rather on account of all this, the greater is the sagacity which provided so solid a foundation for the most important beliefs of man. The subjective Idealism of Berkeley it may be easy for us to refute and explain. Possibly we may find in it a proof of enthusiastic weakness and youthful impetuosity. But his objective spiritualism can never be set aside, while the Theism with which he supplemented science makes itself more and more manifest as a scientific necessity in the confessed judgment of an increasing number of the profoundest thinkers. The positiveness and naïveté with which Berkeley assumes the existence of God, as an axiom in philosophy, may be a scandal to many speculative thinkers; but the history of speculation, especially in more recent times, must demonstrate to a greater number the conclusion that scientific Theism is a philosophical necessity.

At the first thought, it seems altogether incongruous and unseemly to connect Kant or his speculations with Berkeley and his philosophy,— the one is so breezy and sunny, the other so sombre and cloudy; the one is so open and direct, the other is so evasive and remote; and yet the two are more nearly connected than at first sight would seem to be possible, not merely by their historic connection through Hume under the law of action and reaction, but by the problems with which both grappled so earnestly, although their solutions sometimes vary so widely. We find them in certain particulars nearer to one another than we should at first have suspected. The matter which Berkeley so passionately rejects while he retains the sensations which are all we know, is, as he conceives it, not greatly unlike the *Ding an sich* which Kant so pertinaciously ignores, while he accepts the phenomena, which somehow he holds to be its representative. The time and space which Kant acknowledges as *the forms* and only as the forms of our direct knowledge — affirmed or presumed — of sense experiences by an *a priori* necessity, are accepted by Berkeley as *a priori* relations, because necessarily involved in the continued activity of God. Kant's *categories* of our generalized thinking are matched by Berkeley's original notions of relations between the ideas which are discerned and affirmed directly by the mind. The *ideas*, however, which Kant beheld as shivering ghosts through the mists of his timid skepticism and which he was forced to recognize as real by a faith which he could only say was a make-believe, — of God, the soul, and the cosmos, — these were to Berkeley the pillars and foundation of his philosophic faith. While Kant finds in conscience the command to believe in God, because God is needed as a chief of police for the moral universe, Berkeley finds in God the personal foundation and enforcer of duty, because duty is the voice of the reason and goodness, which are but other names for the thoughts and actings of God.

While we may not say of the system of Berkeley that it answers all the questions which philosophy bids us ask, we can say that its answers, so far as they are given, are clear, coherent, comprehensive, and inspiring, while Kant perpetually tantalizes us with solutions which we do not always understand and cannot always accept. It is gratifying to find evidence that the fashion of philosophizing which was set so positively by Kant, gives signs of having worn itself out, and that a new fashion, which is nearer to nature and sanctioned by common sense, is beginning to find currency even in Germany, after which the true Absolute is more and more distinctly recognized as a personal intelligence, the necessary relations of whose self-existence are at once the objects and the elements of a solid philosophy.

NOTE C.— Nothing is more interesting in modern philosophy than the admiration of John Stuart Mill for Berkeley as a philosopher; while nothing is more amusing than the partial and even materialistic applications which he makes of Berkeley's idealistic theory. Mill's estimate of Berkeley as a philosopher is found in one of the last essays * which came from his pen. He says: " We think it will be recognized that of all who, from the earliest times, have applied the powers of their minds to metaphysical inquiries, he is the one of greatest philosophic genius; though among them are included Plato, Hobbes, Locke, Hartley, and Hume; Descartes, Spinoza, Leibnitz, and Kant." In proof of his eminent genius, he finds " three first-rate philosophical discoveries;" "the doctrine of the acquired perceptions of sight;" "the non-existence of abstract ideas;" and "the true nature of the externality which we attribute to the objects of our senses." It is as a representative and champion of Berkeley, in the mutilated form in which his doctrines were modified by Hume,

* Berkeley's Life and Writings. Three Essays on Religion: Henry Holt & Co., 1874.

that he criticizes the philosophy of Sir William Hamilton, confronting his realism with what he calls "the psychological theory," *i. e.*, the theory that resolves the material world into combinations of ideas, after the relations of succession and simultaneity which tend to recall one another under the law of association, and are finally united into enduring complexes, giving the definition of matter as "a permanent possibility of sensations." "This conception of matter," he contends, "includes the whole meaning attached to it by the common world, apart from philosophical and sometimes from theological theories."* This phrase, "the permanent possibility of sensations," in the creed of Mill, covers and expresses all the meaning which we attach to matter as the cause of our sensations. Our confident "expectation," that one sensation will be followed by another, expresses all that we understand or intend by the proposition that one event is caused by another; while the expectation itself is "the product of associations, so often conjoined as to have become inseparably united." Mill agrees with Berkeley so far as to resolve matter as an object entirely into sensations, *i. e.*, ideas, but he fails to agree with him in the judgment that as such a combination, it is produced by the Creative mind. In other words, he has substituted Hume's doctrine for that of Berkeley in these two particulars: first, he dispenses with the creative mind as the objective producer of sensations, and, second, he substitutes inseparable associations with the expectations which they engender for causative relations, both objective and subjective.

In his denial of spirit, creative and human, Mill follows Hume closely and extravagantly, except that he substitutes feelings as psychological in contrast with sensations as cor-

---

* Examination of Sir William Hamilton's Philosophy, etc., Chap. XI.

poreal, whatever this contrast may signify in his analysis. Not content with the denial of the Ego,— in this sharply contrasting with Berkeley,— he follows the steps made necessary by his own analysis, even to the resolution of the Ego into "a permanent possibility of feeling which forms the notion of myself." "The mind is but a series of feelings," "or thread of consciousness," "supplemented by believed possibilities of consciousness," all of which is crowned by the paradox which **Hume never would have ventured to assert,** viz.: that the mind is only "a series of feelings, which is aware of itself as past and future," although he confesses in **the same** breath that this **brings us into** contact with that "final inexplicability" which "belongs to ultimate facts." *

The discerning critic will not need also to be told that, with all the admiration which Mill expresses for Berkeley, he rejects the most **important features** of his system, viz.: God, **as the** originator **and sustainer of the ideas which we call** material, created spirits as the receivers of the same, and the relations between the ideas by which we rise to science. **Whereas Berkeley makes God to be known directly by the mind as the** axiom and corner-stone of all other knowledge, Mill represents Berkeley as giving us a doubtful argument for **his being derived from** and founded on his works. Instead of the Ego, **of which Berkeley insists that we** are directly conscious, Mill gives us a **thread of consciousness** or a permanent possibility of feeling. Berkeley holds that our sensations as ideas of the Divine mind are perpetually renewed by divine agency in the minds of men. Instead of the more or less permanent **associations of the same, by bonds of coexistence, succession, and** similitude, which Mill is compelled incidentally to recognize

---

* *Cf.* Review of Hamilton, Chap. XII. *Cf.* also James Mill, Analysis of the **Human Mind, 2d** edition, Chapters V. and X., with notes.

without finding a place for them in his theory, Berkeley endows man with the original capacity to recognize these relations as elementary and original constituents of knowledge. In Berkeley's own language, "Thing or Being is the most general name of all; it comprehends under it two kinds, entirely distinct and heterogeneous, and which have nothing common but the name, viz.: *Spirits* and *ideas.* * * * We comprehend our own existence by inward feeling or reflection, and that of other spirits by reason. * * * In like manner, we know and have a notion of *relations* between things or ideas; which relations are distinct from the ideas or things related, inasmuch as the latter may be perceived by us without our perceiving the former. To me it seems that *ideas*, *spirits*, and *relations* are all in their respective kinds the object of human knowledge and subject to discourse, and that the term *idea* would be improperly extended to signify everything we know or have a notion of."—Principles, §§ 89, 90.

All this Mill overlooks, accepting only sensations, and half accepting their relations, but finding no place for either the human or divine spirit, as an original agent or ground of knowledge.

The almost contemptuous tone in which Mill speaks of what he calls "Berkeley's argument for the existence of God," as presented in Alciphron, displays a singular misapprehension of the place which the Supreme holds in Berkeley's theory, and of the evidence which Mill requires, and which Berkeley never presumes to furnish of this fundamental element even of such knowledge. That Mill should call this presentation of this great truth an argument would seem to indicate that he failed to appreciate its place in Berkeley's theory of knowledge, and his conception of the essential ground for the inductions of practical wisdom and of instructed science.

The contemptuous disposition which Mill makes of the interpretations given in Siris of the physical and metaphysical theories of the Platonists betrays a singular incapacity to find even any approximations to important truth in the imaginative essays of the great teachers of antiquity. Whatever else may be true of much of the physics and chemistry of this essay, and even of some of its metaphysical suggestions, it cannot be denied that it contains some of the wisest as well as the noblest passages of critical and philosophical wisdom which the English language can show. It would seem as though the admiring reverence in which Mill held Berkeley should have forbidden the expression of his entire disesteem of any portions of his writings, even if it did not lead him to suspect the soundness of his own criticisms.

NOTE D.—The artotype prefixed to this volume was copied from a painting executed at Newport by Smybert which was presented to Yale College in 1808 by Isaac Lothrop, Esq., of Plymouth, Mass. The principal figure is the Dean. The lady with the child is Mrs. Berkeley, and her companion is undoubtedly Miss Handcock. The gentleman writing at the table is Sir James Dalton. The gentleman standing behind the ladies is Mr. James. The one farthest on the left is Mr. Smybert, and the remaining gentleman is Mr. Moffat, his friend. Of some five or six portraits of the Bishop, this is esteemed the best.

NOTE E.—It may seem surprising to many persons that an estate of ninety-six acres in the immediate vicinity of Newport should have been leased for nine hundred and ninety-nine years for so small a rent, and that so much importance should be attached to the foundation of a classical fellowship, of an inconsiderable value, in an institution like Yale College. The estate was rented at first on short leases of a few years, but, as is set forth at great length in the statement of reasons which forms a part of the final lease in 1769, the waste and injury actually suffered by the property, the absence of any reason for believing that its value would be increased, and the expressed desire of George Berkeley, the son of the original donor, induced the corporation to make a perpetual lease of the property as estimated by its then market value.

The significance of this endowment in the history of the college lies in the fact that this was the first endowment for a fellowship for graduate students that is known to have been provided in any American college, and that Berkeley's example is not known to have been followed till after the expiration of a century.

> "How far that little candle throws his beams!
> So shines a good deed in a naughty world.
> —*When the moon shone, we did not see the candle.*"

The Bristed Scholarship, yielding the income of about two thousand dollars, was founded in 1848, is tenable by a graduate student for three years on certain conditions, and the Clark Scholarship became available in the same year, and gives the income of two thousand dollars for two years to a resident graduate. The first Fellowship proper, viz., the Douglas Fellowship of ten thousand dollars, was founded in 1872, and subsequently, in 1883, twenty-five thousand dollars became available by the bequest of Harry W. Foote, as the foundation of one or more fellowships.

In 1875 the Soldiers' Memorial Fellowship was founded by a gift of ten thousand dollars; and, in 1881, the Silliman Fellowship became available by gifts and their accumulation to the same amount. In 1877, four scholarships of five thousand dollars each were founded by the bequest of Mrs. Irene Larned.

From this brief statement it appears that for more than a century Berkeley's endowment was alone in Yale College, and perhaps in this country. From 1733 to 1885 two hundred and forty graduates of the college are known to have been recipients of "the Dean's bounty," or at least to have been elected on examination "Scholars of the House." A nearly complete list of these, prepared under the direction of President Daniel C. Gilman, of the Johns Hopkins University, may be found in The Transactions of the New Haven Colony Historical Society, Vol. I. A hasty glance at their names will discover very many who attained the highest positions in church and state. A superficial knowledge of the literary history of the times will suggest that a special and most honorable prize for special studies in classical learning, in the authors proposed, could not fail to stimulate to a culture which would be felt for the lifetime of every one of these students. During more than a century of this time classical books in good editions could not easily be procured. The careful study of several books of Homer, of a portion of Xenophon, and the Tusculan Questions of Cicero, would leave its impress upon the mind which would never be forgotten, especially in the early days of fewer books and the more complete and permanent mastery of their contents. The authors which had been read would be preserved in the scanty libraries which were then at the command even of the most favored scholars. The successful student would not soon forget that he had derived a special advantage and a distinguished reputation from his classical reading, and would often recur to his old text-books to rekindle the fires of his youthful studies; while he could not fail to bless the memory of the ardent idealist who had founded the fellowship which brought to himself distinguished honor. The writer recollects seeing in his early youth a well-worn copy of the Tusculan Questions, which had been the life-long property of a distinguished Governor of Connecticut who had been a Berkeley scholar. He has an equally vivid recollection of a story told him by a member of the Litchfield county bar of one of his associates, also a "Scholar of the House," who entertained him with a recitation from the Iliad, as long as he would hear him, in a lonely ride in the valley of the Housatonic, the ripple of whose waters was the accompaniment to the well-sounding Greek.

As has been already stated, more than a century elapsed before Berkeley's example was followed, notwithstanding that urgent and oft-repeated appeals were made for the foundation of "terminable fellowships" in our colleges and universities. We cannot doubt that this example will be more stimulating and fruitful in the future than it has been in the past.

PRESS OF THEO. L. DE VINNE & CO. NEW-YORK.

www.ingramcontent.com/pod-product-compliance
Lightning Source LLC
Chambersburg PA
CBHW031123160426
43192CB00008B/1088